FOOTBALL

FOOTBALL: THE DEFENSE

BRYANT LLOYD

The Rourke Book Co., Inc.
Vero Beach, Florida 32964

EDITORIAL SERVICES:
Penworthy Learning Systems

Library of Congress Cataloging-in-Publication Data

Lloyd, Bryant. 1942
Football: the defense / by Bryant Lloyd.
p. cm. — (Football)
Includes index
Summary: Discusses the basics in football defense, covering such aspects as defensive sets and the work of the tackles, the linebackers, and the backs.
ISBN 1-55916-211-2 (alk. paper)
1. Football—Defense—Juvenile literature. [1. Football.]
I. Title II. Series
GV950.7.L543 1997
796.332'2—dc21

97–778
CIP
AC

Printed in the USA

Table of Contents

Riddell

DEFENSE

Football matches one team's **offense** (AW fents) against another's **defense** (DEE fents). The offense has the ball and begins each play. It is the attacking team. It tries to score points.

The defense tries to protect its goal line from the offense. It must always guess what play the offense will run.

The defense can stop the offense by tackling its ball carrier or forcing him out of bounds. The defense can also catch or knock down a pass by the offense.

Early football games were like the English game of rugby. Rugby-style football came to the United States in 1874 from McGill University in Montreal. Colleges in the Eastern United States slowly changed the rules to the modern form of football.

The job of defense is to tackle the offense's ball carrier or force him out of bounds.

Stopping the Offense

The offensive team begins play with a set of four plays, or **downs** (DOUNZ). Play starts from the **line of scrimmage** (LYN UV SKRIM idj). That is wherever the ball lies.

The offense has four downs to gain 10 yards (9 meters) forward from the line of scrimmage.

The defense (white) lines up on one side of the ball with the offense (yellow) on the other side. Neither side can cross the imaginary line until the offense puts the ball into play.

Like bees, defense (black) swarms onto a ball carrier.

If it makes 10 yards (9 meters), it has a new set of four downs. The defense works to prevent the offense from earning new sets of downs.

Taking the Ball Away

If the defense keeps the offense from gaining 10 yards (9 meters) in three downs, the offense usually punts on its final down. A punt is a kick that turns the ball over to the team that had just been on defense.

The defense can also get the ball by picking up a fumble or by making an interception—catching the ball when the other team passes it.

A fumble is a ball dropped by the ball carrier. Anyone can pick up a fumble.

An interception is a thrown ball that a defensive player catches.

A key to good defense and stopping the offense is strong, sure tackling.

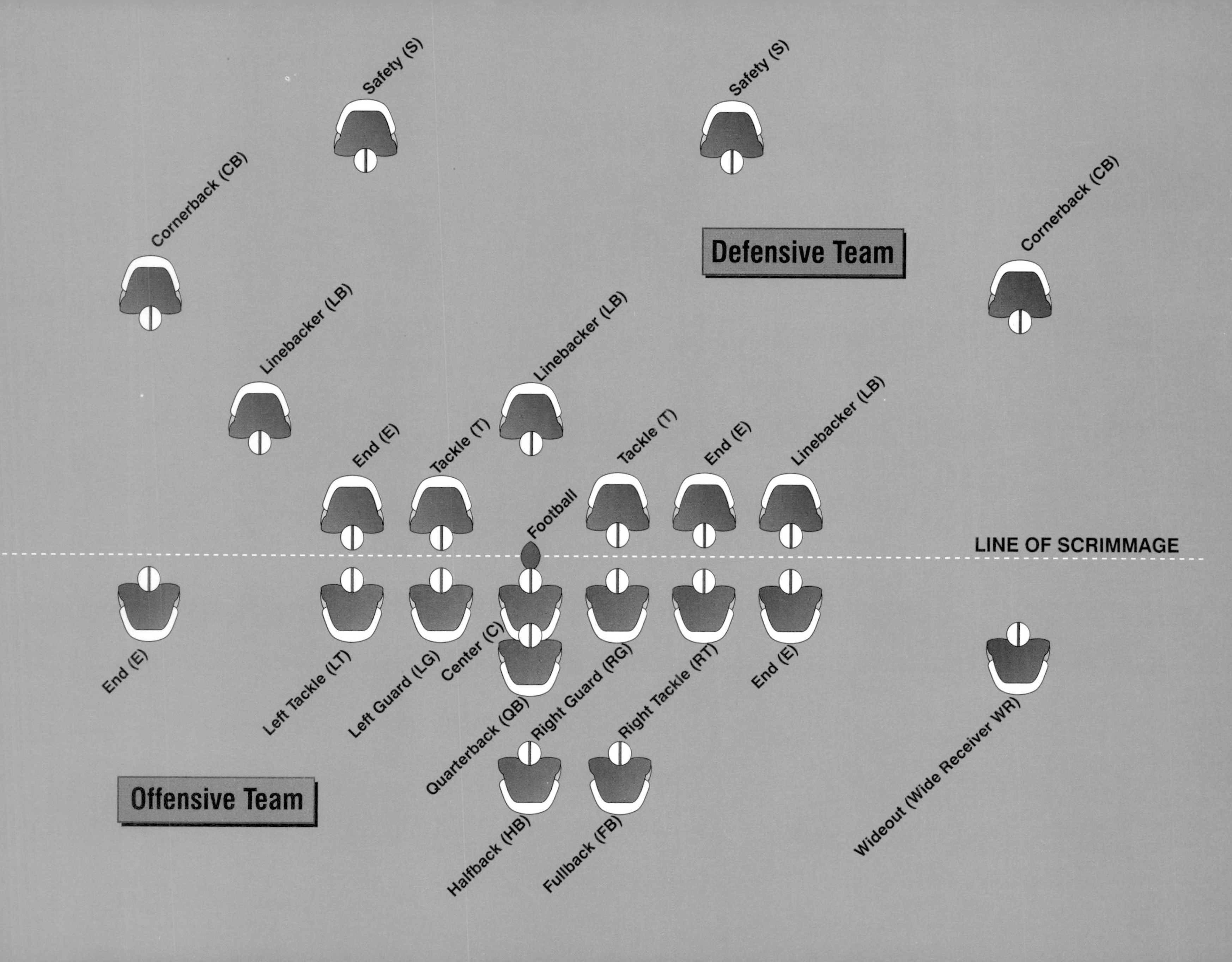
Safety (S)
Safety (S)
Cornerback (CB)
Defensive Team
Cornerback (CB)
Linebacker (LB)
Linebacker (LB)
End (E)
Tackle (T)
Football
Tackle (T)
End (E)
Linebacker (LB)
LINE OF SCRIMMAGE
End (E)
Left Tackle (LT)
Left Guard (LG)
Center (C)
Quarterback (QB)
Right Guard (RG)
Right Tackle (RT)
End (E)
Wideout (Wide Receiver WR)
Offensive Team
Halfback (HB)
Fullback (FB)

Defensive Sets

Defensive players line up opposite the offensive players. Exactly how they set up depends upon several things. How far away is the defense's own goal line? Is it first, second, third, or fourth down? Is the offense likely to pass, run, or kick?

If a defense expects the offense to pass, it will use one kind of set, or defensive formation. It will use other sets if it expects a run or kick.

Each player in the set plays a position. He is responsible for doing certain things.

The NFL (National Football League) began in the early 1920's. College football was more popular than professional football until television brought the NFL into millions of homes in the 1950's.

Diagram shows a defensive set against an offense's formation.

DEFENSIVE ENDS

Defensive ends are the two players at or near the ends of the defense's line. The players on the line are the defense's first wave of defenders.

A good defensive end is strong, smart, and somewhat reckless. He must be able to fight off **blockers** (BLAHK erz).

A defensive end (70) tackles the ball carrier by hitting him low.

Defensive end (center) holds "staying home" position to see how play develops.

His main job is to keep the ball carrier from getting around him. He tries to force the ball carrier back to the inside of the field.

Sometimes the end charges the **quarterback** (KWAWR ter bak). At other times he "stays home," guarding his position against a run.

Nose Guards and Tackles

The nose guard and two defensive tackles are the defense's "inside" linemen. They line up closer to the ball than the ends.

In sets with a nose guard, he lines up opposite the offense's center. The nose guard's job is to push past the center and hurry or tackle the quarterback.

The tackles are named well. They are tacklers and chasers. They have to know who has the ball and go after him quickly.

Unlike offensive linemen, defensive linemen can use their hands to push and pull.

Bowl games match college football teams in December and January. Bowl games are played by teams that finish their regular seasons with good records.

Defensive tackle (52) lunges toward quarterback, who has just thrown football.

GOLDEN EAGLE
52

Riddell
66

Linebackers

Most defensive sets use two outside linebackers and a middle linebacker. They form the defense's second line of defenders.

Linebackers tend to be tough, hard-hitting players. Although big and strong, they are usually smaller and quicker than linemen.

One job of linebackers is to meet and tackle the ball carrier if he breaks through the linemen. Linebackers also have to be alert for passes.

Linebacker (66) hustles to meet ball carrier.

Defensive Backs

A defensive set usually has four backs—two safeties and two cornerbacks. They form the defensive secondary, the defense's last line of defenders.

Backs are the smallest and fastest defensive players. They are also tough tacklers.

Defensive backs often find themselves one-on-one against the ball carrier. Sure tackling is a must for defensive backs.

The receiver (yellow jersey) makes the catch, but defensive back is there to make the tackle.

Defensive backs guard the offense's fastest pass **receivers** (ree SEE verz). If the receiver catches the ball, the back must be nearby to make the tackle.

Defensive backs often catch or knock down passes that are meant for the offense's receivers.

The Blitz

Defensive sets change to meet the changing situations of the game. Sometimes the defense changes its set so quickly, it fools the offense.

With a blitz, for example, the defense sends more players than usual to rush the quarterback. A cornerback may suddenly charge from his position into the offense's backfield.

He takes a risk. By leaving his usual position, the cornerback cannot defend against a receiver there. The cornerback gambles that he can reach the quarterback before the quarterback can throw to a receiver.

Tackle football is played in the United States by more than 14,000 high schools. More than 700 colleges and universities field football teams, too.

The quarterback was surprised by the blitz of a defensive back.

PANTHER
2

GLOSSARY

blocker (BLAHK er) — an offensive player who makes physical contact with a defensive player to stop or slow him

defense (DEE fents) — the team that is protecting its goal line against the team with the football

down (DOUN) — any one of the plays run by a football team from the line of scrimmage

line of scrimmage (LYN UV SKRIM idj) — an imaginary line across a football field; place where the ball is put after a play

offense (AW fents) — the team with the ball; the team that puts a football into play

quarterback (KWAWR ter bak) — the offensive team's player who calls plays and directs the football

receiver (ree SEE ver) — any player who catches a forward pass; one who sets up in a football formation as if he might catch a pass

Teamwork in the form of gang tackling stops a ball carrier.

INDEX